CANDID MOMENTS

For When You Just Need a Little Bit of Jesus

VALERIE DENOR

Candid Moments

For When You Just Need a Little Bit of Jesus

Copyright © 2021 by Valerie Denor

Cover design by Heather Hart

Cover photo © Galina Peshkova | Deposit Photos

About Candidly Christian

The mission at CandidlyChristian.com is to be open and honest about our faith and our struggles while we encourage other women in their walk with God. Our hope is that we can come together to love one another as Jesus loves us. **Candid Christianity is all about real women, with real faith, sharing real life.**

We would love to hear from you! You can send comments, questions, and prayer requests to the following address:

Candidly Christian

C/O Heather Hart

P.O. Box 1277

Seymour, TX 76380

Or connect with us online!

Email: heather@candidlychristian.com

Twitter: @CandidGals

Instagram: CandidlyChristian

Facebook: CandidlyChristian

Table of Contents

Dedication

I dedicate this book to my friend Natalie Killion. Natalie, for years I've planned on dedicating my first book to you because without you, not a single word would have been published. Thank you for supporting me and believing in me, even when no one else did. Without you to keep my head up, and even to resuscitate me from time to time, I would have drowned in life's storms many years ago and ten times over. Thank you for being the truest reflection of unconditional love I've ever known. Thank you for being you.

Hugs,

Valerie

Introduction

Heather planned on getting four days' worth of work done that morning, in between basketball practice, grocery shopping, and dentist appointments. The mid-morning phone call wasn't unusual, but it stopped her in her tracks.

Her husband had left a few things in the backyard that couldn't weather an on-coming storm. As she glanced out the window, it was more than a tool here and there that needed her attention. The kids' toys lay scattered over the yard as well.

Of course, she would pick them up. She didn't even think twice about it. Gray clouds hovered overhead as she set about her task, finishing her new assignment before the first raindrops hit.

When she came back inside, the phone rang again. Someone else needed help only she could provide. The task would kill any chance that she'd get everything done that day. Hanging up the phone, Heather glanced over at the table where her Bible still lay open from her quiet time that morning, and she wondered, "How can the Gospel fix this?"

At that moment, Candid Moments was born.

Candid Moments are brief devotionals designed to encourage you in those moments when you just need a little Jesus to calm the storm.

We all face storms in life.

We all get stressed out and overwhelmed.

We all have bad days.

Just as a single raindrop can lead to a flood, so it is with our thought life. But what if we stop the rain before it washes us away?

Each of the following devotions came out of my own storms. Some storms felt like tornadoes, where all I could do was scream out His name in the sudden chaos. Sometimes I could hear the thunder rumbling for miles, so I had time to prepare through prayer and Scripture. Others were more like pop-up showers in the middle of an otherwise sunny day, so I just asked Jesus to cover me with His wisdom like an umbrella. But no matter what the situation, or how poorly I was handling it, He responded with exactly the shelter I needed and walked through the storm with me.

He wants to do the same with you. My hope with Candid Moments is to help you focus on Jesus and keep your eyes above the waves. You'll be able to read each devotion in about the time it takes to put on a jacket. If you want to be prepared for the next tornado or you're sitting through a hurricane, I've also provided space throughout the book for drawing, prayer, or journaling. One day, my journaling consistent entirely of writing Jesus's name over and over because that's all I could handle at that moment. He answered me then, too, and He'll answer you every time you call on Him for a life preserver.

1

The Storms of Life

But when he saw the wind, he was afraid, and beginning

to sink he cried out, "Lord, save me."

Matthew 14:30

The other day I saw a graphic on Facebook of Jesus standing on the water during dark and stormy seas. In the background, the caption said *Focus on Me*.

When you're in the storm, are you focused on Jesus?

The Bible says that when Peter focused on Jesus, He gave Peter both peace and dominance over the storm that were beyond understanding. But when Peter focused on the storm again, his capabilities were just like everyone else. He was terrified and helpless.

The storm is going to rage matter what. Are you going to sit in the boat paralyzed with fear? Or are you going to focus on Jesus so He can give you His peace and ability to handle the storm in a better way? I need to remember this when my storms rage, and I hope it encourages you.

Prayer

Jesus, I need You to walk through life's storms with me, because without You, I'll sink. Please call me back and remind me to focus on You when my attention wanders. Thank You for Your peace and wisdom, and please help me continue to grow closer to You every day. I love you, Jesus. Amen.

2

Serenity

Then Jesus told his disciples, "If anyone would come after me, let him deny himself and take up his cross and follow me."

Matthew 16:24

God, grant me the serenity to accept the things I cannot change; the courage to change the things I can; and the wisdom to know the difference.

Don't we love the Serenity Prayer? Like iced tea under the scorching sun, it's so refreshing during hard times.

And like that tea, doesn't it seem like your soul is parched again just moments after those sweet words have left your lips?

I love the Serenity Prayer, too, but I believe it's missing something. You see, God doesn't just grant peace, courage, and wisdom like a genie in a bottle. He's about relationships, not magic, and prayer is active and powerful, so we must be active participants.

It took me a long time to understand that I can't just say a few fancy prayers to make all my troubles melt away. I'm learning that serenity comes from surrendering my controlling spirit and giving my cares to Jesus in prayer. I find courage by trusting our All-knowing God who loves me. And I find wisdom by reading His Word.

God isn't a genie in a bottle, but He is our comfort for every crisis.

He won't wave all your troubles away upon demand, but He shares the answers to all of your questions in the Bible.

I won't pretend it's easy or that I've got it all figured out, because it's not and I don't. But I know that it's easier leaning on Jesus's infinite strength and wisdom than the shallow reservoir of my heart.

We all need serenity, courage, and wisdom, especially in uncertain or challenging times. Every day, every hour, every minute if necessary, call out to Him and join me in prayer.

Prayer

Jesus, I give this to You. You're in charge, and I trust You because I know You love me. I don't understand what's happening, but the one thing I know for certain is that You never change. Thank You for giving Your life to make Your serenity, courage, and wisdom available to me. Please help me trust You more. I love You, Jesus. Amen.

3

Resist

Submit yourselves therefore to God.

Resist the devil, and he will flee from you.

James 4:7

The devil tempted Jesus repeatedly as He wandered through the desert for forty days. Each time, Jesus resisted Satan's bait and instead obeyed God's plan, until eventually the devil fled.

I struggled with debilitating anxiety for a long time, because I was afraid to confront Satan and call him out on his lies. But when I learned that Satan is defeated by the Blood of the Lamb[i], Jesus reminded me I am covered by that same blood, and that I belong to Him.

So now when the enemy tries to bait me with fear and worry, I plead the blood.

How do I do this? I find a place where I can be alone, open my mouth and talk right back at that dirty lair! I remind Satan that not only is he already whopped, but that I'm covered by the same blood that whopped him. Then I put on Jesus's armor and put Satan on notice that I belong to Jesus, so he has to go through Jesus to get to me.

Prayer

Jesus, I'm struggling, but I know You are with me. Satan, I'm calling you out. Your are nothing but a defeated liar! I am covered by the blood of Jesus, so I belong to Him! He defeated you, so that means you have no power over me, either. Get out and leave me now! Jesus, thank You for saving me both now and for eternity. I claim Your peace and wisdom. Thank You for claiming me as your child. I love You, Jesus. Amen.

4

Opportunity

Carry each other's burdens,

and in this way you will fulfill the law of Christ.

Galatians 6:2 NIV

As Christians, we are ready and waiting to obey Galatians 6:2 and provide prayer and help to one another. But we sometimes forget that there are two active parties in this verse.

I recently went through a hurtful situation that left me mentally and emotionally frozen. I needed help, but we're all struggling with different things, and I didn't want to burden anyone with my issues.

Paul's instructions to the Galatians assume that we'll reach out when we're overwhelmed. As my dad always said, "We can't fix what we don't know is broken." My problem was mine to fix, but it's also my responsibility to recognize when I need help and to be humble enough to ask.

I reached out for help that day. My friends and family provided prayer, comfort, and wisdom, so I got back on my feet much faster than I would have alone.

Are you overwhelmed today? I invite you to ask someone for comfort and prayer and give them the opportunity to fulfill the law of Christ.

Prayer

Jesus, I'm overwhelmed, and I need help. Please tell me who I can reach out to today to hear wisdom and encouragement from another believer. Please also show me when I can help carry another person's burden. Thank You for the Christians in my life. I love You, Jesus. Amen.

5

New Beginnings

He put a new song in my mouth, a song of praise to our God. Many will see and fear, and put their trust in the LORD.

Psalm 40:3

We know King David as a man after God's own heart, a giant slayer, and the author of ancient psalms. But David also went through a lot of hardship. His brothers taunted and underestimated him, Saul's army hunted him for years, and his own son betrayed him, just to name a few life-altering challenges he overcame.

When I had cancer, I couldn't wait for treatment to end so I could get back to my normal life. But so much happened, I couldn't go back to my previous life. Instead, I had to navigate a new normal.

I found encouragement in a card from a dear friend that said "God is a God of New Beginnings." I also held on to Psalm 40:3, written by King David after God delivered him from hardship.

Instead of wishing for the life I lost, I learned to praise Jesus for the life He delivered me from. As I did so, His peace replaced my sorrow, and I looked forward to my new tomorrows.

Now I point others to Jesus by sharing what He's done for me. And I wouldn't trade that for anything!

Are you adjusting to a new normal? Perhaps you're mourning the comfort and familiarity you can't get back. If so, I encourage you to move forward in praise for the God of new beginnings.

Prayer

Jesus, sometimes I struggle to see the good I this, but I know You are always with me. Thank You for Your comfort and strength. Thank You for new beginnings. Please help me adapt. Please show me how to use this to point others to You. I love You, Jesus. Amen.

6

Closer

And we know that for those who love God all things work together for good, for those who are called according to his purpose.

Romans 8:28

I finished cancer treatment one year ago. As I reflect on how Jesus used cancer to draw me closer to Him and to heal my anxiety, it seems like the experience happened to a different woman in another life.

I'm reminded of a Romans 8:28, a scripture the enemy uses to turn many people away from God. I'd already been walking in my calling, sharing Jesus's peace online for two years before cancer. So why did I get cancer at all? Certainly, cancer isn't for my good!

In the moments after my diagnosis, I vowed to stand against anxiety by leaning on Jesus. But I didn't want to share my experience publicly until my husband proposed I write about my struggle to help other women draw closer to Jesus.

In that moment, God used my husband to call me according to His purpose: drawing me and other women closer to Him.

Jesus never promised everything would go smoothly for His followers. In fact, in the moments before He ascended to heaven, He promised we would all have struggles, but to have faith in Him.

Jesus's purpose was to reunite mankind with the Father, and so this is our calling, too. No matter what you're going through, things can work together to bring you and those around you closer to Jesus. This is your calling, if you choose to accept it.

Prayer

Jesus, this is hard, but I know You are with me. Please use this situation to bring me closer to You. Please also use me to bring others closer to You so that, even at my weakest, they'll see Your strength. When I wander, please remind me that my hope and strength are in You. I love You, Jesus. Amen.

7

The Lord Our Banner

And Moses built an altar and called the name of it,

The Lord Is My Banner.

Exodus 17:15

As Americans, we rally behind our flag. Old Glory represents the history, beliefs, and strength of our nation. We stand to honor our banner of stars and stripes because it represents who we are.

One of my favorite Old Testament stories is the Israelites' battle against the Amalekites in Exodus 17:8-16. Moses took the staff God gave him at the burning bush, and Aaron and Hur joined him to watch the battle from a hilltop. The Israelites prevailed only as Moses held up God's staff in his hand. Whenever Moses put his hand down, the Amalekites prevailed, so Aaron and Hur supported his arms and helped him keep the staff held high.

The Israelites won the battle because they fought with the staff of God—a visual of His faithfulness and might. After the battle, Moses built an altar to the Lord and called it *The Lord is My Banner.*

What enemies are you fighting today? Are discontent, self-doubt, or bitterness threatening the peace of you and your household? Are you battle weary from trying to hold it all together by yourself for too long? When I get anxious and frustrated, I find peace in Scripture, prayer, and by asking for support.

I encourage you to rally behind the Lord your Banner. When you put your faith in Jesus, and let other believers lift you up in prayer, you have the faithfulness and strength of the Almighty God behind you. You're guaranteed to succeed in this battle because Jesus already won the war.

Prayer

Jesus, I've been in this battle for a while and I'm getting tired. Please send someone to lift me up. Please show me how I can reach out to and ask for help and prayer. Thank You for giving me strength through You and others. Thank you for the power of prayer. I love You, Jesus. Amen.

8

Take Heart

Jesus said the words in verse John 16:33 during the Last Supper. I used to hear Jesus's encouragement to His disciples and think, "Good for You, Jesus. What's that got to do with me?" But now I know that the same power that overcame the world also lives in His believers.

Sometimes, I think the world is a scary and confusing place. So often I say to my husband, "I just don't understand this world anymore. People confuse me and nothing makes sense." In moments of confusion and fear, God's children can choose to turn from fear and instead embrace the all-knowing Almighty God.

Even in a passing moment, we can cast our cares on Jesus. God gave us His Holy Bible, the Basic Instruction Book for Living on Earth, so we can seek His peace and His will in Scripture. The same God that overcame the world died to give you and me the power and wisdom to live in it. You can't raise yourself from the dead, but you can lean on the one who did.

Prayer

I'm confused and afraid, but I give this to You, Jesus. It's out of my control, but I know You are in charge and I trust You. Thank Your for Your peace. I love You, Jesus. Amen.

9

God's Gifts

Most of us are familiar with the book *The 5 Love Languages* by Gary Chapman. He wrote that we all express love in the same way we feel love from others, whether it's through spending time together, physical touch, kind words, acts of service, or gifts.

Did you know God expresses His love for you in the same ways? But how do you feel God's love from day-to-day if your love language is giving and receiving gifts? As if God will show up in your living room with His hands behind His back, teasing, "Guess what I've got you!?"

I've always known that God loves me, but His love felt distant until the day I learned how to recognize the little gifts He gives me every day.

It was the summer when my daughter was four years old. Like many girls that age, she loved dandelions, and like most mothers, I loved nothing more than to receive a freshly picked mittful of the bright weeds from our backyard to display on the kitchen table!

As soon as my husband pulled into the driveway after a weekend of camping, I saw it—the biggest, brightest, tallest dandelion I'd ever seen. A single splash of color reaching for the clouds from a crack in our driveway.

The flower wasn't there before we left just two days prior, but now it stood proud, almost six inches tall. As my daughter squealed and jumped out of the car, I knew there was only one way that lone dandelion could have grown so tall overnight, and I thanked God for the gift of the flower and for my daughter's delight.

Have you considered that perhaps you don't know how your Heavenly Father shows you His love every day? Did you catch a glimpse of elusive wildlife today? Maybe someone helped you or gave you the encouragement you never told anyone you needed. Did you spot just the item you needed at the store, and on sale just after you'd given up looking?

Some might call it coincidence. But as God's children, we know nothing happens without His knowledge. When we pay attention, we'll notice His gifts of unchanging love all around us, every day.

Prayer

Dear Jesus, thank You for both the big and small the gifts You give me every day. I'm sorry sometimes I don't recognize it's You. Please help me recognize and appreciate the love You give me. I love You, Jesus. Amen.

10

Sowing & Reaping

Do not be deceived: God is not mocked, for whatever one sows,

that will he also reap. For the one who sows to his own flesh

will from the flesh reap corruption, but the one who sows

to the Spirit will from the Spirit reap eternal life.

Galatians 6:7-8

You acted in love, so how did things end so badly? How are you going to save your beloved prodigal now? I've been through the heartbreak of rejection from a prodigal that didn't want to be saved. Even during rejection, I still spent my energy to either prevent or clean their mess.

But Scripture said I had to let go.

As Christians, we want to look out for one another, but there are some things we have to do for ourselves. I can't choose Christ as your Savior for you. You can't give an account for my choices before God.

And we can't reap what a prodigal sows, no matter how much we love them. God has ordained that those who sow to his flesh will reap corruption, and when I try to get in the way, I'm making a fool of God.

It's hard to turn away and let their decisions run the natural course, but I find peace in giving my loved one to Jesus in prayer every day. Are you struggling with a wayward loved one who doesn't want to be saved? Seek God's direction in prayer and Scripture. It's possible it may be time to get out of the way, to let God do the work in their heart that only He can.

Prayer

Jesus, I'm so concerned. Please show me what do to and please tell me if I'm supposed to stay out of the way and let You work. I know You love them even more than I do, and You will work everything for their good when they are ready to seek You. Please give me peace during the wait. I love You, Jesus. Amen.

11

Constant

Jesus Christ is the same yesterday and today and forever.

Hebrews 13:8

Greek philosopher Heraclitus first said, "The only thing constant is change." But Heraclitus lived 500 years before Jesus. Sometimes life changes so fast, I feel like I don't know where or even when I am anymore.

Uncertainty is hard because without knowledge, we have no control. We feel helpless, anxious, and fearful. It's true that change is constant, but it's not the only constant we know for certain. Jesus Christ is the same yesterday and today, and forever. What does this verse mean to you and me as we struggle through change?

It means that no matter what the question or the conflict, Jesus is the answer.

No matter how much it seems like there's no way out, Jesus is the way maker.

When your foundation is shaken, He is still your rock.

Even as leaders fail, the Son of God is still the King of Kings.

If you dread the dawn, know that Immanuel is with you and goes before you.

When you feel alone, remember El Roi is the God who sees you.

As darkness overcomes you, raise your eyes and your voice toward the Light.

Are you lost? Let the Shepherd lead the way.

And when you're anxious, leave your cares at the cross of the Prince of Peace.

Benjamin Franklin once said, "Nothing in this world can be said to be certain—except death and taxes." But he, too, was wrong.

I can show you certainty, but only if you surrender control of your tomorrows to the one with the answers. It's in the Bible. It's on the cross. It's in your next prayer.

The Good Book is not a crystal ball. Prayer is not a magic spell. Change, death, and taxes all await after you unfold your hands and put the Bible back on the shelf. But if you lay down your will to obey His Word, you'll have Jesus's peace, wisdom, and strength to guide you.

Prayer

Jesus, this is happening so fast, and I don't know what to do or how to adapt. I trust You, Jesus, so I give my fear to You. Please show me how to adjust and give me the grace to change. I love You, Jesus. Amen.

12

Christ in Me

I have been crucified with Christ. It is no longer I who live,

but Christ who lives in me.

Galatians 2:20a

Whenever I felt insecure, my Grandpa Gordon would chuckle and drawl out in his endearing Rocky Mountain accent, "Well, you're part of me, see, so you've gotta be good."

Grandpa Gordon was one of the most gentle and loving men I knew. I was proud to be a part of him, and his approval empowered me. When Grandpa Gordon died, each of us five kids insisted we were his favorite. We all knew that he was proud to call us his grandchildren, and he loved us unconditionally.

And so it is as children of God. In the Book of Galatians, Paul tells us that Jesus shares much more than our bloodline. As His chosen child, you share His mind, His soul, and His heart. And He loves you so much that He gave His life to call you *Mine*.

Are you feeling inadequate today? I'd encourage you to open your Bible and speak to Jesus in prayer. Learn and remember who you are as His child and let Him empower you in His love.

Prayer

Jesus, thank you for dying to save me so I could be part of You. Please forgive me when I forget who I belong to. Please help me live so people will see You in me. I love You, Jesus. Amen.

13

Seeking Jesus

And he said to them, "Why were you looking for me? Did you not know that I must
be in my Father's house?"

Luke 2:49

The Passover Festival was so busy! So many people, so much going on. Mary had only taken her sight off Jesus for a few moments. Then suddenly, she realized He was gone! Can you imagine the panic, the nauseating fear? What kind of mother loses the Son of God?

But yet, don't we all lose sight of Jesus every single day?

I've always found the first recorded words of Jesus a bit peculiar. But I knew His opening statement had to be significant. When I read this story again last week, Jesus wasn't speaking to His earthly parents. Instead, He asked me: "Why were you looking all over for Me? Didn't you know I would be doing my Father's work?"

Sometimes Jesus feels far away, but He's always been in the same place. It's you and I who wander. He's amid His creation. You'll see His reflection in a smile, a comforting hug, or a random act of kindness.

Do you feel alone, like God has forgotten you? Jesus Christ is the same yesterday, today, and forever, so He's right where you left Him. He's waiting for you to return from your wandering. The Word *is* God, so open it. Jesus gave His life to be one with you, His beloved chosen child. All you have to do is call His name in prayer.

Prayer

Jesus, I feel lost and alone and I miss You. I'm sorry I've wandered and forgotten about You. Thank You for always being there, waiting for me. Please help me stay close to You every day. I love You, Jesus. Amen.

14

Covet

You shall not covet your neighbor's house. You shall not covet your neighbor's wife, or his male or female servant, his ox or donkey,

or anything that belongs to your neighbor.

Exodus 20:17

King Ahab was so obsessed with Naboth's vineyard that when Naboth wouldn't sell the property, he went home to bed and pouted. Queen Jezebel told her husband to grow up, but then she unleashed her own adolescent attitude of noble entitlement. And Naboth's homicide brought upon the wrath of God and her own family's gruesome demise.

I think God included "thou shalt not covet" in the Ten Commandments because He knows we're inclined to become obsessed with what we can't have. Eve did it in the Garden of Eden long before King Ahab. I pouted for several years when lifesaving surgery left me unable to have the big family I'd always wanted.

My grandpa used to say, "I felt sorry for myself because I had no shoes until I met a man who had no feet." They say you can judge a man by his shoes, but God judges the heart. So instead of letting desire morph into idolatry, I'm learning to confess my sin and give thanks to the God who gave us everything we need in His Son Jesus.

Prayer

Jesus, You gave your life for me, yet I still want more. I'm sorry for being ungrateful. You are all I need, and I thank You for Your provisions. Please help me better follow Your commandments. I love You, Jesus. Amen.

15

God's Will

God, Your Word says we can ask for anything in Jesus's name and for Your glory. I can't see it yet, but I'm coming to you in His name, with faith and trust in Your promises that it will come to pass, so I thank you now Father, for answering my prayer...

Have you ever prayed like this, only to feel disappointed and betrayed?

When my most urgent prayers weren't answered, I felt forgotten and abandoned by God. When I asked Him why He didn't come through on His Word, He showed me that "name-it-and-claim-it prayers" are founded on a list of scriptures taken entirely out of context. The promise comes with the condition that we are asking according to God's will to do His work, and for His glory.

But how do we know if we're asking according to His will?

I found the answer in Matthew 22:37-38. God's will is for us to love Him, and each other, with all our heart, soul, and mind. Jesus's name isn't our speed dial to divine room service. But He is the only way to the Father.

I'm learning to surrender my own circumstantial agenda for His ways, and to pray for joy, peace, patience, kindness, faithfulness, goodness, and gentleness in every circumstance. And when others ask me where my strength comes from, I point them to Jesus.

Prayer

Father, I'm sorry for treating your Son like waiter. Thank you for helping me better understand and pray for Your will. Please continue to help me embrace Your desires as my own. And this I ask in Jesus's name. Amen.

16

Can You Handle It?

God is faithful, and he will not let you be tempted beyond your ability, but with the temptation he will also provide the way of escape,

that you may be able to endure it.

1 Corinthians 10:13

The assurance that God will never give me more than I can handle almost made me turn from Him. Many days I've felt so desperate that I wanted to give up, and the idea that my circumstances came from God, and that I was expected to be strong enough, was more than I could bear.

First Corinthians 10:13 seemed to confirm that I was both weak and a disappointment to God, but I knew this didn't align with God's character, so I studied the verse to find the truth.

So, is it true that God doesn't give you more than you can handle?

Yes.

And no.

First Corinthians 10:13 doesn't say God will not allow suffering. It says He will not allow you to be tempted without a way out. Temptation is an invitation to sin, and we always have a choice.

The truth is that suffering is a natural consequence of sin, both our own and someone else's. God doesn't give trials; He uses them to bring us closer to Him.

All good things come from God, and His character never changes. The only way to eliminate sin and trials is to revoke our autonomy, and God loves us too much to turn us into His puppets. Are you struggling with temptation or unsure of how to handle a difficult situation? I encourage you to ask Jesus to show you the way out.

Prayer

Jesus, thank you for loving me enough to give me a choice to turn from sin and the choice to live by Your Word. And thank you for loving me even as I sin. Please help me walk in Your ways. I love You, Jesus. Amen.

17

Look Up

Jesus said to her, "Woman, why are you weeping? Whom are you seeking?" Supposing him to be the gardener, she said to him, "Sir, if you have carried him away, tell me where you have laid him, and I will take him away." Jesus said to her, "Mary." She turned and said to him in Aramaic, "Rabboni!" (which means *Teacher*).

John 20:15-16

I remember one dark morning when I sat on the floor in our basement, surrounded by a pile of tissues again. I held my head in my hands, trying to catch my breath, when the most unlikely of songs began playing in my head.

It was Lauren Daigle singing "Look up child, eh hey." I ignored her and blew my nose again to drown her out, but she just wouldn't be quiet. It was then that I realized it was God speaking to me through music, as He often does. So, I lifted my head, looked up at the ceiling panels and whispered, "Jesus, help me."

My favorite part of the Easter story is when Mary is too busy crying at the empty tomb to realize Jesus is standing right in front of her. Mary gets me. But the most incredible part is that a hot mess of a woman like me was the first to see the risen Lord. Jesus didn't choose royalty or a calm Bible scholar to appear to first. He chose a woman who came running to find Him.

What I've learned from Mary (and Lauren Daigle) is that Jesus is always with us. All we have to do is look up.

Prayer

Jesus, thank You for loving me just where I am. Thank You for being there for me at any hour, whether I'm seeking You or acting like I don't know You. Please help me remember to always keep my eyes on You, especially when all I want to do is hang my head. I love You, Jesus. Amen.

18

Pray Together

So from now on we regard no one from a worldly point of view, though we once regarded Christ in this way we do so no longer. Therefore if anyone is in Christ, the new creation has come:

the old is gone, the new is here!

2 Corinthians 5:16-17

Have you ever prayed with a stranger and then instantly felt a unique, lasting connection with that person? Did you wonder why you felt such a fondness for someone for whom you spent so little time?

I recently attended my first 3-day virtual writers retreat. The weekend was so Spirit-led that it felt more like a prayer retreat. I woke up Monday morning feeling thoroughly fulfilled, totally exhausted, and lonesome for my new sisters in Christ. I wondered how could I feel such fondness, such genuine love for women I barely knew.

Later that week, 2 Corinthians 5:16-17 showed me how Christian friends are different because we don't regard one another from the worldly view of regular acquaintances. Christians are new creatures in Christ, and nothing brings this to life more than coming to Jesus together in prayer. By coming together in the Spirit, we are then connected in our spirit.

Are you feeling alone today, even as you're surrounded by others? I encourage you to find a prayer partner, and you'll see how coming to Jesus together will remind you that you're never alone.

Prayer

Jesus, thank You for the special connection of prayer. Thank You for empowering my little prayers to grow closer to You and other Christians. I'm so grateful to know I'm never alone. I love You, Jesus. Amen.

19

Fearfully Made

I praise you, for I am fearfully and wonderfully made.

Wonderful are your works; my soul knows it very well.

Psalm 139:14

When I first started reading the Bible, I gravitated to scriptures about my identity in Christ. Looking back, I know my recovery from debilitating anxiety had to begin with learning who God says I am. But honestly, Psalm 139:14 didn't help, because all I heard was that I was scary. I've never understood how so many people could cling to a verse that said we were fearfully made, so I focused on the other, prettier verses.

But recently God brought me back to Psalm 139:14 as I read Shannon Popkins' book, *Comparison Girl.* As Shannon explained our worth as God's beloved daughter, she wrote, "Our worth is not up for evaluation. [ii]"

The words leaped into my heart so forcefully that I had to put the book down and just sit. Those seven words marinated and simmered in my mind for days, along with God whispering, "You are fearfully and wonderfully made."

It turns out the original Hebrew word for *fearfully* isn't the scary kind of fear at all. It's the reverent, astonishing, remarkable kind of fear. The jaw-dropping kind of fear that makes you stand in awe and wonder. In fact, other translations of Psalm 139:14 capture this. My favorite is the *Holman Christian Standard Bible*, which says "I will praise You because I have been remarkably and wonderfully made. Your works are wonderful, and I know this very well."

What I love even more about Psalm 139:14 is that it praises God for His wonderful works. So, it's not really even about me, it's about praising God. If you're beating yourself up today, I encourage you to praise Him for the astounding, breathtaking love and thought He put into creating you perfectly for your exact time, place, and purpose.

Prayer

Jesus, thank You for creating me perfectly to carry out Your will. Please help me continue to grow closer to You so I can help others see the wonderful work You've done in them. I love You, Jesus. Amen.

20

When Trouble Comes

Cast your burden on the LORD, and he will sustain you;

he will never permit the righteous to be moved.

Psalm 55:22

One day, a close friend shared her struggles with a situation we have in common. When she asked me how I can have such peace over my particular circumstances, I told her, "I pray it away," and then immediately realized how trite that sounds to someone who is hurting. So, I confessed, "Sometimes I don't have peace at all. I had a few bad days recently. But when that happens, it doesn't last as long or get as bad because I take it to Jesus."

Jesus promised we will have trouble in this world, so struggles aren't a matter of *if*, but *when*. Psalm 55:22 reminds us of Jesus's promise to be there for the ones He made righteous on the cross. When you lay your burdens at the cross of the one who overcame the world, your hurt can't overcome you. The one who carried the cross also carries your pain and lifts you up.

Prayer

Jesus, I'm carrying a burden today. It's too heavy for me, but not for You. I lay this burden down at Your feet, Lord. I surrender my fears and hurt to You. Thank You for making me righteous and for lifting me up. I love You, Jesus. Amen.

21

Feeling Failure

We can rejoice, too, when we run into problems and trials,

for we know that they help us develop endurance.

And endurance develops strength of character,

and character strengthens our confident hope of salvation.

Romans 5:34 NLT

I eagerly signed up for the writing challenge and committed to write a devotion every day. I announced to the group what a perfect opportunity this is to make progress on my book.

During the first week of the month-long challenge, I didn't write any devotions, but I took my material out, refreshed my memory on where I'd left off, and re-invited Jesus to write with me. It was a start, even though I didn't make the progress I'd hoped for. But at check-in after the second week, I publicly reported a word count of zero, a giant goose egg. The challenge was half over, and I'd failed to write a single devotion.

I wallowed in my failure for a day or two, ready to give up, until Scripture reminded me that there is no such thing as failure for the believer, because God uses my shortcomings to give me an opportunity to endure so I can become stronger and more confident in Him.

God knew all along that I'd bomb the writing challenge. He also knows that I can choose to persevere. Yes, word counts are important because books only get written as you put words on the page. But what's even more important than the word count is the journey of becoming a little more like Jesus.

Are you looking in the mirror and seeing disappointment looking back? I invite you to take your weakness to Jesus in prayer. Receive His strength and love to persevere and grow a little closer to the hope and future He has planned for you.

Prayer

Jesus, I'm feeling like a failure, but I know you're never disappointed in me. Your Word says there is no condemnation for those who love You, so I give my disappointment to You, Lord. Please use this experience to help me learn, grow, and become a little more like You. I love You, Jesus. Amen.

Valerie's Testimony

Thank you for reading my book. To be honest, it was Heather's idea to include my testimony at the end. I prayed on what to write for weeks, mainly because Jesus keeps writing my story day by day. Of course, the past doesn't change, but the lessons do as the years go by, and there are always new lessons. So, I decided to focus on the part that never changes: my brokenness and Jesus's goodness.

I was raised Catholic as the oldest of five kids on a traditional family farm in Wisconsin. I was baptized as a baby and attended church nearly every Sunday in a 250-year-old chapel that was only recently updated with the luxury of a port-a-potty fitted with a lock on the door.

I knew Jesus died to give us His peace and so we could have an abundant life on earth until we meet Him in heaven. But after a series of illnesses, my heart was full of anything but peace and life. I finally understood why anxiety had such a grip on me one day one day at church when the choir sang, "Let your faith run free across the raging sea and walk across the water to Me." I realized my relationship with Jesus was on the shore, and I needed to find freedom in the Living Water He talked about.

But seriously, I already believed in Jesus. Why wasn't that enough?

Believing in Jesus is about more than head knowledge, and that's where I was. I mean, even the devil knows Jesus is real. Believing is about flooding your mind with so much Jesus that His peace surges into your heart. It's about knowing Him so intimately that you put your faith and trust in Him.

An intimate relationship requires investment, so I had to make the effort. That's the knocking and seeking the Bible talks about. Fortunately, Jesus doesn't play hard to get. He was waiting for me in prayer and Scripture, even when I was afraid of being played the fool or setting myself up for another letdown.

In time, I learned to trust Jesus because He went to the cross and back to prove He'll never leave me, all the while knowing I will let Him down, again, and again, and again. I've learned that freedom through Jesus means stepping out in faith and trust, especially during the storms, to surrender my control by His feet at the cross.

Victory comes only through surrender to Jesus.

That's my story and my message. It's a lifestyle I walk out by holding Jesus's hand every single day.

Before I started writing, I'd get a little star-struck when a writer replied to my comment online. Now that I'm an author, I can tell you we love nothing more than to hear from our readers. Writing requires a certain vulnerability, especially in the faith niche. But we do it out of obedience to our calling, trusting that God will use our heart's sacrifice for His purpose.

I tell you this so you know it's not just social etiquette when I say, "hearing from you will make my day." But if you never reach out, that's totally okay. Either way, I pray that when you come to Candidly Christian, you will always leave knowing this:

You are not alone.

You are loved.

There is always hope in Jesus.

Notes

About Valerie Denor

After suffering years of debilitating anxiety, Valerie learned that victory over anxiety comes only through surrender to Jesus. Valerie walks in her calling to use her words for Jesus as the founder of Faithful Pen Ministries, where she serves as a writer, collaborator, editor, and biblical mentor. Valerie lives in Wisconsin in a cozy, riverfront apartment with her cat, Maizie. You can learn more about Valerie at https://www.faithfulpen.com/.

Like This Book?

❖ Join the movement by sharing your struggles and using them to point to Jesus—be sure to tag them with #CandidlyChristian on social media.

❖ Write a book review on Amazon, your blog, and/or another online retailer.

❖ Join our Facebook group facebook.com/groups/candid conversations[1]

❖ Visit our website, CandidlyChristian.com, where women get candid about their life and faith every week.

❖ Tell your friends and family about this book.

---

1. http://www.facebook.com/groups/candidconversations

More Candid Moments

Candid Moments:

God is Good, Even When the Struggle is Real

Heather Hart

Red Letter Candid Moments:

Because Their Moments Are Our Moments

Valerie Denor

Candid Moments:

For When You Need Jesus to Help You

Keep Your Eyes Above the Waves

The Candid Gals

Also Available

Candid Conversations

Life isn't always sunshine and chocolate. It's hard.

In *Candid Conversations,* you'll hear real-life struggles that real Christian women have faced head-on, and how God has either used those struggles to refine their faith or used their faith to help them weather the storm. From struggling with doubts to dealing with the loss of a loved one, these women lay it all out. They aren't afraid to get real, because they know God can use their struggles to inspire, encourage, and reach others all for His glory.

[i] Revelations 12:11

[ii] Popkin, Shannon. Essay. In *Comparison Girl: Lessons from Jesus on Me-Free Living in a Measure-up World*. Grand Rapids, MI, MI: Kregel Publishing, 2020.